D0819914

FAMILY MATTERS

You and Your Parents' Divorce

Katherine Krohn

the rosen publishing group's
**rosen
central**

For Gerard Alcantara

Published in 2001 by The Rosen Publishing Group, Inc.
29 East 21st Street, New York, NY 10010

Library of Congress Cataloging-in-Publication Data

Krohn, Katherine E.
   You and your parents' divorce/by Katherine Krohn.—1st ed.
        p. cm.—(Family matters)
   Includes bibliographical references and index.
   ISBN 0-8239-3354-7 (lib. bind.)
      1. Children of divorced parents—Juvenile literature. 2. Children of divorced parents—Psychology—Juvenile literature. 3. Divorce—Psychological aspects—Juvenile literature. [1. Divorce.] I. Title. II. Family matters (New York, N.Y.).
   HQ777.5 .K76 2000
   155.44—dc21
                                                                        00-010494

Manufactured in the United States of America

Contents

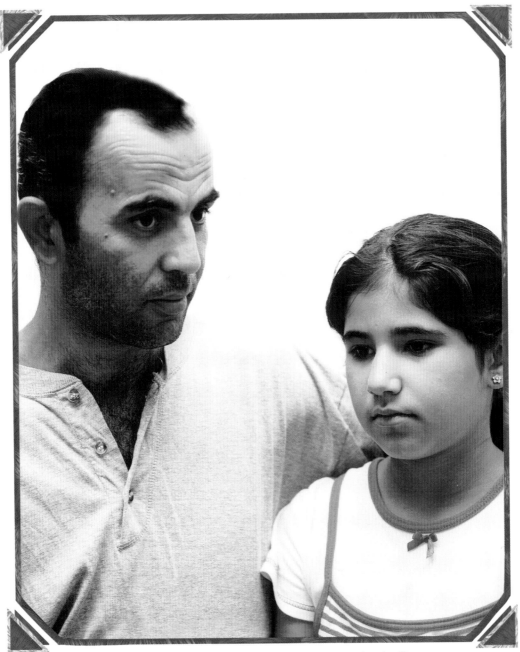

Divorce brings life changes and emotional challenges to everyone in the family.

Introduction

"Last Saturday morning, my sister and I were watching a video when mom and dad came in the room and asked us to turn off the television. Then my dad said, 'Your mom and I are getting a divorce,' " says Giovanni, fourteen, a New Jersey middle school student.

"My mom started to sob, and then my little sister started to cry, too. My heart raced and I felt like I couldn't breathe. I couldn't believe that this was happening.

"My dad said, 'We still love you. . .we want what is best for you both. Your mom and I still love each other, but we just can't live together.'

"I got so mad. I told my dad that what he had said didn't make sense—I mean, I thought married people were supposed to stick with

each other, no matter what. My dad tried to hug me, but I pulled away from him.

"Then my mom flew off the handle. She yelled to my dad that she didn't want a divorce, and she didn't want her children to think that the divorce was her fault. She screamed that it was my dad's fault they were getting divorced. My dad yelled at her to 'grow up,' and they just kept yelling at each other. I felt sick to my stomach."

Chances are, you know someone whose parents are divorced. Or maybe your own parents are divorced or are planning to get a divorce. If so, you know firsthand how difficult the changes that come with a divorce can be.

This book is written for people like you who are going through a hard time because of divorce. This book will help you sort out your feelings, understand the divorce process a little better, and point you in the right direction to seek out further help.

What Exactly Is a Divorce?

A divorce is the legal separation of a husband and wife. A divorce happens when two married people decide that they can't live together happily anymore. The man and woman sign legal papers which end the marriage. Once single, they are free to marry someone else if they want to.

Divorce brings life changes and emotional challenges to everyone in the family. Kids of divorce often have to adjust to new routines. Mealtime and homework routines can change. Sometimes kids have to move when their parents divorce. They may have to attend a new school or live in a new home. Relatives and friends who were once close may be farther away.

YOU ARE NOT ALONE

If your parents are getting divorced, you may think that you are the only kid who feels like you do. In reality, the opposite is true! Studies show that close to 50 percent

If your parents split up, you are hardly alone—50 percent of marriages end in divorce.

of marriages in the United States end in divorce. While everyone's personal story is different, "kids of divorce" know how you feel. You are not alone.

Kids of divorcing parents may feel as if they are on an emotional roller coaster—with frequent, stomach-churning ups and downs. They may feel angry, sad, rejected, confused, guilty, or even ashamed.

"Whenever you feel overwhelmed or ashamed about your parents' divorce," says author Rachel Aydt, "remember that you are not a freak who is living through something so horrible, bizarre, and upsetting that no one else can relate to your situation. More people than you can imagine have already lived through this."

WHEN DIVORCE IS A POSITIVE THING

Although divorce can seem like the worst thing in the world, it can sometimes be for the best. Living in a

Not All Change Is Bad

The changes that come with your parents' divorce can be uncomfortable and upsetting. But your parents' divorce can bring you positive changes, too, such as:

◇ Growth
◇ Independence
◇ Inner strength

◇ Learning
◇ New experiences
◇ Wisdom

family where your parents don't get along and argue frequently can cause a lot of stress and anxiety. Silent wars—when parents don't fight, instead preferring to ignore each other—can be harmful, too. Even though your parents may not be yelling, they still may not be getting along.

Not all kids feel upset or sad when their parents divorce. Some kids even feel relieved. Montana State University researcher Chelsea Elander asked kids how they really felt about their parents' divorce. "The overwhelming comment was, 'Don't stay together if you are not happy. . .We don't want to live in that environment.'"

"Parents that remain married 'for the sake of the children' may, for all intents and purposes, be emotionally divorced," says social worker Gayle

It is normal to feel confused and even angry about your parents' divorce.

Peterson. While Peterson believes that married people should try to work through marital problems before they consider divorce, she doesn't believe that divorce is always "bad" for a family.

FEELING CONFUSED IS NORMAL

"My dad said, 'You'll have to make some decisions about who you want to live with,'" says Giovanni. "And my mom said that we might not have any choice—like, we will have to live with her. I think she said that just because she's mad at my dad. I have never felt more confused. I don't know who I want to live with. I feel like this isn't really happening, like this couldn't be happening."

It is normal to feel confused about your parents' divorce. In fact, it is normal to feel whatever emotions you are experiencing. You may have a friend whose parents are getting divorced who is moody and cries a lot. On the other hand, you may feel angry and anxious. There are no wrong reactions to a divorce. Regardless of what kinds of emotions you are experiencing, it is important that you know that you can and will get through this challenging time in your life.

Divorce won't ruin your family—it will just change your family.

It's Not
Your Fault

"*I got caught shoplifting a couple of times last year,*" *says Monica, a thirteen-year-old from Michigan. "It caused a lot of tension at my house. Last month, my mom and dad separated. They hired a lawyer and the 'divorce ball' is rolling. I can't help but think if I had stayed out of trouble, maybe my parents would still be together."*

IT'S JUST NOT TRUE!

Often kids of divorcing parents think that they did something to cause their parents' divorce. But divorce is never a child's fault. Here are several common misconceptions, or untruths, that kids have about divorce:

> ◇ My parents are divorcing because I'm a bad kid.

Try to do fun things that will take your mind off your parents' divorce.

◇ It was probably my fault that my parents split up.

◇ If my parents leave each other, they will leave me, too.

◇ If I act extra good, my parents might get back together.

◇ If I act up and cause trouble, maybe my parents will get close again.

◇ My parents stopped loving each other. I guess they will stop loving me, too.

Try to remember that your parents' divorce is about your mom and dad's relationship. Your parents split up with one another—not you or your siblings. Some kids hope that acting like the ideal child will bring their parents back together. For the same reason, others behave badly, hoping that their parents will come together to deal with the problems they are creating. However, bad behavior will only make things worse for you and your parents. And acting like a perfect child won't help either.

THINGS TO KEEP IN MIND

Your parents will be your parents for the rest of your life. Divorce won't ruin your family—it will change your family. When you are upset and feeling hurt or vulnerable, it is especially important to take good care of yourself. Here are some examples of nice things you can do for yourself:

◊ Go for a walk or a bike ride.

◊ Listen to your favorite music.

◊ Read a good book or your favorite magazine.

◊ Hang out with some friends.

◊ Watch a movie.

If you find it difficult or even impossible to talk to your parents about their divorce, try talking to a counselor instead.

Finding Friends Who Understand

When your parents divorce, your emotions can seem overwhelming. You don't need to face your feelings alone. Talk to someone you trust. Ask your parents to set aside time to talk to you about the divorce. Tell them what you are feeling. Explain your concerns. Try to listen to what they have to say, too. The divorce isn't easy for them, either. Some kids find it difficult or even impossible to talk to their mom and dad about divorce. In that case, they may want to find someone else to talk to, too.

TALKING WITH A COUNSELOR

"My parents weren't exactly great communicators, to say the least," says Diddy, sixteen, from Toledo, Ohio. "A friend of my mom's gave her the number of a family therapist. Thank goodness she called that number.

Counselors, psychologists, and social workers are trained to help you work through personal problems.

The therapist helped all of us—my mom, dad, younger sister and me—talk to one another. I know this sounds weird, but we couldn't talk to each other about the divorce before we saw the counselor. We were closed up, and all we did was walk around the house like zombies and watch television."

Counselors, psychologists, and social workers are professionals who are trained to talk to people about their problems. They can help you and your parents communicate with one another. You might want to talk to the counselor alone, too. Counseling can help you talk about, express, and sort out your painful feelings.

OTHER OPTIONS

You could also talk to a trusted adult, like a favorite relative, teacher, neighbor, school counselor, or nurse. Or consider talking to your coach, minister, or rabbi. Also, some kids find it helpful to talk to their peers. Do you have a friend whose parents are divorced? It feels good to relate to people who understand what you are going through.

Luckily, there are helpful organizations all over the world set up just to help kids deal with divorce and other tough issues. Many of these agencies create peer support groups—groups where kids can talk to other kids about divorce.

Nora, thirteen, joined a support group for kids of divorce at her school. "My parents separated when I was very young," she says. "In some ways, it was good, because they used to argue a lot. But it was bad, too. Mom wanted me to live with her, and dad wanted me to live with him. No matter what I decided, one of my parents would be unhappy. What was I supposed to do? Then my grandpa died suddenly. It seemed like one day I knew who my family was and then every-thing changed. People kept telling me it was going to get better, but how did they know?

"In my support group, I learned that none of what happened was my fault. It was good to talk with someone without worrying that what I said would upset my parents. Best of all, when I talked about how I felt or explained what had happened, no one ever interrupted or teased me. Sometimes we just sat and cried together."

Charitable organizations, churches, and social agencies often sponsor programs, such as peer support groups, that help kids deal with family changes.

RAINBOWS

Rainbows is an organization that works with schools, churches, and social agencies to form peer support groups for children and teens dealing with the pain of divorce, death, and other family changes. There are more than 8,000 Rainbows groups in the United States and sixteen other countries.

Roma Downey, star of the TV show *Touched by an Angel*, is the honorary chairperson of Rainbows. "Change can be frightening," says Downey. "It is particularly difficult for children who don't understand what's happening. Grieving children need caring, trustworthy, and knowledgeable adults to whom they can turn. Rainbows teaches that the pain of loss doesn't have to hurt forever."

"Before Rainbows, I was angry all the time—at school, at home, and with my friends," says a Rainbows participant. "Since then, I have learned better ways to let my anger out without getting into trouble. I have also learned to live with what happened. I can accept the changes that have occurred in my family and I feel more confident about my life."

THE INTERNET

On the Internet, there are many chat groups and message boards just for kids and teens to talk to one another about divorce and other issues.

Jade, fifteen, attends a middle school in Indiana. "My parents got divorced when I was seven," she says. "I never thought it bothered me that much. I felt like I could handle it, like I was Superwoman or something!

"About three years ago, I discovered an Internet chat group for kids of divorce. I realized that I never talked about my feelings about the divorce because I was embarrassed. I felt like no one would understand. On-line, nobody knew who I was and I could talk freely. I discovered feelings that I didn't even know I had.

On-line resources—like chat rooms and message boards—can help kids cope with divorce.

"I talked to kids about how we've used our parents, who feel guilty about having gotten a divorce, to get stuff that we want, like new computer games and clothes. I learned that manipulating my parents isn't cool. I recommend Internet groups to my friends whose parents are divorced. I tell them how it makes you feel better, even if you didn't know you felt bad in the first place!"

Jade's best friend, Daisy, fourteen, also found help on-line:

"For years after my parents divorced, I kept my feelings bottled up. Then, after Jade told me about this chat group, I logged on, too. It amazed me how people who had never met me could be so helpful and supportive. Really nice kids from all

over the world gave me all sorts of good advice. I made a lot of on-line friends. I'm very grateful for the Internet."

WEB SITES AND HOTLINES

The University of Illinois has an excellent Web site for kids and teens of divorce. At this Web site, kids can connect with each other and talk about their issues and feelings. This site and others are listed in the Where to Go for Help section at the end of this book.

> **Be Cautious**
>
> When using the Internet, *never* give a stranger (or a new on-line friend) personal information such as your last name, address, or phone number. Choose any on-line chat group or club carefully. Select a site that has a good reputation.

There are many telephone hotlines for young people who need to talk about divorce and other difficult issues. The hotline operator is a caring, helpful professional. He or she can talk to you about your problems and give you feedback and guidance. Some kids prefer to call hotlines to talk about their feelings because they can remain anonymous—the hotline counselor doesn't need to know your real name in order to be able to help you.

Please Don't Put Me in the Middle

Annabelle, fifteen, lives in Maine. Her mom and dad divorced three years ago.

"Whenever my parents would talk to each other, they would get in a big fight," says Annabelle. "Then they quit talking to each other completely. After that I became the messenger—'tell your mother this' or 'tell your father I said blah blah.' What am I, their secretary or something? And I wish they wouldn't talk about each other when I'm around. They usually talk about each other to someone on the phone, and I overhear the conversation. Don't they realize I have ears? It makes me so angry!"

WHEN IT'S TIME FOR YOU TO SPEAK UP

Divorced parents often make the mistake of talking about their ex-spouses within earshot of their children.

If your divorcing parents put you in the middle of their fights, don't be afraid to speak up for yourself.

They do this because they are angry and feel justified in putting down their ex. However, it is not okay for one parent to talk negatively about your other parent in front of you. If one of your parents says something rude or negative about your other parent, don't try to block out what you heard or pretend that it doesn't matter. Tell your mom or dad that you overheard him or her, and ask him or her not to talk about your other parent when you are around. Tell him or her how that behavior makes you feel. If your parent makes the mistake of asking you nosy questions about your other parent, it's time to speak up.

MOM: So, Jasmine, is your dad seeing anyone these days?

JASMINE: Mom, I don't feel comfortable answering that kind of question. If you want to know what dad is doing, please ask him yourself.

Tell your parent that you feel uncomfortable relaying information about your other parent. Ask them to please talk to your other parent directly. Remember, parents are still learning, too. Express yourself. You will feel better, and, hopefully, your parent will learn a lesson.

Finding the Right Words

Sometimes it helps to have planned out what you want to say before you talk to your parent about your feelings. That way, you won't be at a loss for words. Heather gets very angry when her mom puts down her dad. But how can she tell her mom how she feels without making the situation worse?

HEATHER: Mom, it hurts me, and makes me angry, when you talk about dad, because I love him, too. Please don't talk about him around me.

MOM: I didn't realize that it bothered you, Heather. I'm sorry—I guess I wasn't thinking. I won't do that anymore.

I Feel So Angry!

It is normal to feel anger and other intense feelings when your parents are divorcing, but there are both destructive and healthy ways to express anger. It is important to release your anger in ways that won't hurt you or anyone else. Some examples of destructive ways to show anger are hitting someone, breaking a window on purpose, or hurting yourself. A healthy way to express anger is to scream into a pillow or hit the ground with a stick. Jogging or swimming can also release angry tension.

"One thing to do with anger is to use it to make a difference," says Lynn Namka, author of *How to Let Go of Your Mad Baggage*. "Take positive action with the momentum that anger gives. Life is about choices. You have choices about what to do when you get mad," says Namka.

Namka hosts a Web site called "Angries Out," just for helping kids of divorce handle their anger. The Web site is listed in the Where to Go for Help section at the back of this book.

 5 Adjusting to Change

Sometimes kids have to go to court with their divorcing parents. If you have to go to court, you may have to speak to a judge. He or she will help your parents determine the best living arrangement for you and your siblings. Every family's post-divorce arrangement is different, but it is most common for a child to live primarily with one parent and visit the other.

"I have two homes. I have a room at my mom's house and a room in my dad's apartment," says Justin, thirteen. "I have a special calendar that I use to keep track of the days I spend at each of my parent's places. It can get confusing otherwise."

JOINT CUSTODY

Joe is a California middle school student. Since his parents' divorce a year ago, he and his sister, Rose,

Stress can sometimes result when you have to divide your time between your parents' separate households.

eleven, spend half of their time with their father, and half with their mother. This common legal arrangement is known as joint custody.

When a judge declares that a mom and dad will have joint custody of their children, it means that the children will share their time equally between both parents. The parents will share care and responsibility for the children.

Joe's sister, Rose, doesn't really like the split-household arrangement.

"It makes me sad that we're not a family anymore. At least, that's how it feels. Nothing is the same. I miss our old family," says Rose. "It feels so weird to go to my 'dad's place.' It feels wrong."

SOLE CUSTODY

Occasionally, a judge will award custody to one parent. The other parent may or may not have visiting rights. Li Way, thirteen, was ten when her parents divorced. Her father remarried within months, and moved to another state. A judge awarded Li Way's mother sole custody of her daughter.

"I miss my dad, and I don't understand why he moved so far away," says Li Way. "It seems like he just cares about his new wife and stepson. I feel like I don't measure up. Everything has changed so much."

SINGLE-PARENT HOUSEHOLDS

Kids who live in single-parent households often get extra responsibilities. Their busy parent—not only a full-time parent, but often employed outside the home—usually needs extra help around the house.

Gilly's parents divorced when she was nine. Her dad got a job in another state. Gilly, now fifteen, has only visited her dad three times in the past six years. Gilly's mom basically raised her by herself.

"Because I grew up in a single-parent family, I was given lots of extra responsibilities," says Gilly. "Since I was ten years old, I've been doing my own laundry and bagging my own lunches for school. I even cook dinner most nights, when my mom has to work late.

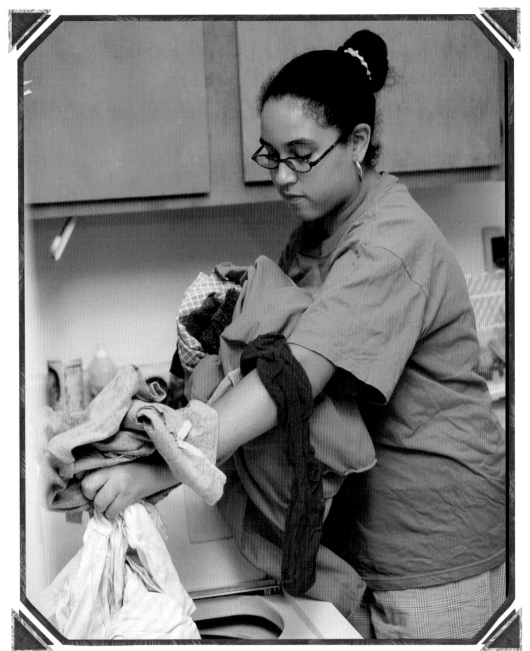

Kids who live in single-parent households are often very independent because they are used to taking on extra responsibilities.

In a way, I don't think it was fair that I had to take on so many grown-up type responsibilities. But I can see that these chores and extra duties made me a more disciplined and trustworthy person. My mom trusted me to do a good job, to take responsibility, and I did."

A Tough Choice to Make

"My mom assumes that both my sister and I are going to choose to live with her, but I'm not," says Juan, sixteen. "My sister told me that she wants to live with my mom, but I don't want to. I want to live with my dad. But I don't want to hurt my mom's feelings. I hate feeling like I'm choosing between them—as if I like one of them better or something. It's not like that. I feel so sad."

Sometimes kids get to choose which parent will be their primary caretaker. This can put kids in an awkward and even painful position. You may feel as if you are choosing sides. You may even feel like you are betraying a parent. But you are simply making a decision based upon what seems right for you right now. It's natural to want to spend time with both of your parents, or to have preferences that shift. For instance, you may at first prefer to live with your mom. A couple of years later, you may choose to spend more time at your dad's place. It doesn't mean that you love one parent more than the other.

You may not like a parent's new boyfriend, girlfriend, or spouse at first, but try to give that person a chance.

LIVING TWO LIVES

Splitting your time between both of your parents can be hard. And long-distance, split-custody arrangements can be especially tough on kids. Nick's parents divorced when he was five. His parents made a split-custody arrangement. He would spend the school year with his father, and summers and long holidays with his mom.

"I began flying between two cities and two different lives. I've probably earned enough frequent flyer miles for a round-trip ticket to Mars," Nick told Newsweek in *an article about divorce.*

"I remember the last day of school in sixth grade. I hated saying good-bye for the summer. It was

easier to put up a wall, to pretend I didn't care. Arriving in L.A., I was excited to see my mom and stepdad. It had been almost three months since my last visit. But it took a while to adjust. Each set of parents had different rules, values, and concerns. I am sixteen now and I still travel back and forth, but it's mostly up to me to decide when. I've chosen to spend more time with my friends at the expense of visits with my mom. . .I'm always missing somebody. When I'm in northern California, I miss my mom and stepdad. But when I'm in L.A. . . . .I miss my other set of parents and little brother and sister."

HELP, MY DIVORCED PARENT IS DATING!

In time, parents may begin seeing new people and dating again. This can be hard on kids, especially when they still have secret hopes that their parents will reunite.

"It was so hard when my parents divorced," says Jefferson, thirteen. "And things are still difficult. My mom has a new boyfriend, and he and I do not get along. My mom and I used to be best friends, but now we are almost like strangers."

Jefferson's brother, Dean, twelve, is also upset that his mom has a new boyfriend.

"When my mom told us that her boyfriend was moving in with us, I couldn't believe it," says Dean. "When she told me, I thought I would go crazy. Not so much because I didn't like her boyfriend, I just didn't want her to be this serious about him. And I feel like my mom will pay less attention to me and my brother now."

STEPPARENTS AND STEPFAMILIES

Eventually, your divorced parent might meet someone new and remarry. If that happens, hold onto your hat and take a deep breath—more big changes are coming your way. You will have a new stepmom or stepdad. And, if your stepparent has children, you will gain stepsisters or stepbrothers, too.

"At first, I didn't like my stepmom, Latifa, at all," says Betty, a fourteen-year-old middle school student from Detroit whose dad remarried two years ago after Betty's mother died. "Latifa really bugged me, and I refused to listen when she told me to do my homework or go to bed. I guess I gave her a hard time. She took some getting used to, but now I think she's kind of cool. She's a lot mellower than my dad and she has taught me a lot of cool stuff, like how to play the drums, read tarot cards, and make gazpacho."

Stepfamily situations can be harmonious and happy. But, sometimes, getting along with a stepparent or stepsibling can be challenging. Personalities can clash, and conflicts can arise.

Michael, seventeen, a San Francisco teenager, was shocked when his dad remarried only a few months after his divorce. Though Michael's primary caretaker is his mother, he visits his dad, and his new stepmother, two or three weekends a month.

"Right off the bat, my stepmom didn't want to have anything to do with me," says Michael. "I'm not exaggerating—she doesn't like kids. I heard her tell my dad that she thinks kids are slobs. She's a neat freak, and

It is normal to have mixed feelings about a new stepparent.

her (and my dad's) house is spotless. I have no idea why my dad married her in the first place. I've learned to tolerate her. When I visit, my dad and I go off and do stuff and she stays at home. The situation is totally weird, but I try to get along with her because I love my dad."

How Can I Get Along with My New Stepparent or Stepsibling?

"I have really mixed feelings about my stepfamily," says LeeAnne, a middle school student from Pennsylvania. *"But there are good things about living in two houses, too. I have a cat and a fish at my mom's. And at my dad's house I have a dog, a kitten, and a lizard. My dad remarried, so I have a stepmom, too. But I also have a stepbrother, Doug, who's very mean and bossy. We get into fights and he grabs my things, and because he's much taller and stronger, I can't get them back. Then he just laughs at me. I can't stand him! My dad says I can't hit my stepbrother or even yell at him. He says I will have to adjust, but I don't want to. I only stay at my dad's place every other weekend, but, because of my mean stepbrother, I dread going to my dad's place sometimes."*

About American Children
United States Divorce Statistics

◇ One in two children in the United States will live in a single-parent family at some point in childhood.

◇ One in three children is born to unmarried parents.

◇ One in four children live with only one parent.

◇ One in twenty-five lives with neither parent.

Does your stepparent or stepbrother or sister do something that makes you really angry? Are you having a hard time dealing with conflicts between your stepsibling and yourself? If you don't work at resolving issues with your stepfamily, your problems will only continue. Conflicts should be resolved in a peaceful way. Fighting will only make things worse.

Talk to your stepparent or stepsibling, and tell them your feelings. Tell them how you want the situation to change. You may also want to talk to your mom and dad when stepfamily issues come up. When working out conflicts, it helps to work toward a compromise instead of a victory. Try to meet the other person halfway. If you try, you will probably find that there are peaceful solutions to the problems you are having.

Time for a "Pow Wow"

LeeAnne decided to talk to her dad about her issues with her stepbrother, Doug. She tried to stay calm as she explained everything. She told her dad how Doug's behavior was making her not want to visit his house. Her dad listened, and then he called the whole family together for what he called a pow wow—a family meeting. At the meeting, LeeAnne told Doug exactly how his actions made her feel. Doug said he had just been trying to make her laugh, and he hadn't been trying to hurt her feelings or make her feel bad. He agreed to treat LeeAnne with more respect.

"I felt so relieved after we all talked," says LeeAnne. "I'm not 100 percent sure my stepbrother will really stop being mean, but I'm willing to give him another chance. Things do seem better already."

CHANGE BRINGS GROWTH

Remember Giovanni, the New Jersey middle school student mentioned at the beginning of this book? When Giovanni received the news that his parents were getting a divorce, he felt like his world was caving in. He was totally overwhelmed with confusing and painful emotions.

"My little sister and I spend weekdays with my mom and weekends with my dad," reports Giovanni. "My dad lives in this cool apartment complex that has an indoor heated pool. It's fun to go to his house. Of course, I miss us being a family, but I've accepted the fact that that is impossible.

"My dad is dating again. I dread the possibility that he might remarry someday, even though I like the woman he's dating. It's just too much change, you know? But I've learned that everything doesn't go smoothly all the time. I try to make the best of things and be helpful. I think everything will be okay."

Change of any kind can be a challenge, and your parents' divorce can be one of the greatest challenges you will face in your life. Change brings you into unfamiliar territory.

Divorce can be tough, but don't worry—you'll survive.

Change can be scary. But you can also see change as an adventure—as an opportunity to learn and grow and take on new experiences. If you can do this, you will have a smoother and more rewarding journey.

Maybe you can't change your parents and make them married again, but you can change your attitude. You can choose to accept the divorce and not let it get in the way of your having a happy life.

As you go through your parents' divorce, try to be helpful to your parents and other family members. Be sure to ask for outside help when you need it. There are people who understand the feelings you are having, and they want to help you. Sometimes the ride will be a little bumpy, but you are going to be okay.

Glossary

alimony (or spousal support)   Financial support payments made to a spouse after a divorce.

child support   Money paid by a parent, after a divorce, for the care of the children.

divorce   The legal ending of a marriage.

joint legal custody   Legal arrangement in which parents share decision-making about the care of the child.

joint physical custody   Arrangement in which the child or children divide time between both parents after a divorce.

marriage   Legal and/or religious union of two people.

noncustodial parent   Parent with whom the child does not live after a divorce.

separation   When parents decide to live apart from each other. A "trial separation" lets them see what it is like not be married anymore. Some parents get back together after a separation.

sole custody   Arrangement in which one parent has complete responsibility for the child or children. Custody establishes with which parent a child or children will live after a divorce.

support group   Group of people who agree to meet regularly to discuss a common issue and support one another emotionally.

visitation rights   Legal rules about how often noncustodial parents may see their children.

Where to Go for Help

IN THE UNITED STATES

Children's Defense Fund
25 E Street NW
Washington, DC 20001
(202) 628-8787
e-mail: cdfinfo@childrensdefense.org
Web site: http://www.childrensdefense.org

Rainbows
2100 Golf Road
Rolling Meadows, IL 60008-4231
(800) 266-3202
Web site: http://www.rainbows.org

Stepfamily Foundation, Inc.
333 West End Avenue
New York, NY 10023
(212) 877-3244
Web site: http://www.stepfamily.org

In Canada

Canadian Youth Rights Association
27 Bainbridge Avenue
Nepean, ON K2G 3T1
(613) 721-1004
Web site: http://www.cyra.org

Family Service Canada
404-383 Parkdale Avenue
Ottawa, ON KIY 4R4
(613) 722-9006

Hotlines

Banana Splits Support Group
(212) 262-4562

Childhelp
(800) 422-4453

Covenant House Nineline
(800) 999-9999

NEO Teenline
(800) 272-TEEN (8336)

Youth Crisis Hotline
(800) 448-4663

WEB SITES

Angries Out
http://members.aol.com/angriesout

Divorcing.com
http://www.divorcing.com

iConnect: Dealing with Divorce
http://web.aces.uiuc.edu/iconnect

My Two Homes
http://www.mytwohomes.com

Sandcastles
http://www.sandcastlesprogram.com

For Further Reading

Aydt, Rachel. *Why Me? A Teen Guide to Divorce and Your Feelings.* New York: Rosen Publishing Group, 2000.

Bianchi, Anne. *Understanding the Law: A Teen Guide to Family Court and Minors' Rights.* New York: Rosen Publishing Group, 2000.

Hart, Archibald D. *Helping Children Survive Divorce: What to Expect, How to Help.* Nashville, TN: Word Publishing, 1997.

Johnson, Linda Carlson. *Everything You Need to Know About Your Parents' Divorce.* New York: Rosen Publishing Group, 1999.

Johnston, Janet R. (ed.). *Through the Eyes of Children: Healing Stories for Children of Divorce.* New York: Free Press, 1997.

Joselow, Beth B., and Thea Joselow. *When Divorce Hits Home: Keeping Yourself Together When Your Family Comes Apart.* New York: Avon Books, 1996.

Sullivan, Steve. *Confessions of a Divorced Kid.* Ridgefield, CT: Motivational Resources Book, 1996.

Wilson, Jacqueline. *The Suitcase Kid.* New York: Delacorte, 1997.

Index

About the Author

Katherine Krohn is the author of several books for young readers, including *Everything You Need to Know About Birth Order*, *Everything You Need to Know About Living On Your Own*, *Women of the Wild West*, *Rosie O'Donnell*, and *Princess Diana*. Ms. Krohn is also a journalist and fiction writer. She lives in Eugene, Oregon.

Photo Credits

Cover and interior shots by Ira Fox.

Design and Layout

Geri Giordano